HYPNOSIS ESSENTIALS:

POWER UP YOUR LIFE!

Presented by

Marlene Shiple, Ph.D.
The Life Coach Dr.
http://thelifecoachdr.com/coach
(602) 266 - 6662

HYPNOSIS ESSENTIALS:

POWER UP YOUR LIFE!

Published by Approaches to Coaching, Unlimited, Press
Phoenix, AZ. 2010

<u>Dedication</u>

To my Loving husband, Glenn,
who enhances my life with delight,
inspiration, and understanding!

HYPNOSIS ESSENTIALS:
POWER UP YOUR LIFE!

*"There are only two ways to live your life.
One is as though nothing is a miracle.
The other is as though everything is a miracle."*

-- Albert Einstein

HYPNOSIS ESSENTIALS: POWER UP YOUR LIFE!

TABLE OF CONTENTS

"Too frequently, we have already been hypnotized

– via conditioning in infancy or in early life –

to believe ideas about ourselves that are untrue!"

-- Dr. Lena Cather

HYPNOSIS ESSENTIALS: OVERVIEW OF HYPNOSIS

Hypnosis is a state in which the body is relaxed and the mind is alert and aware. The process of hypnosis involves a hypnotist and a subject (a person on whom hypnosis is performed). For hypnosis to be successful, the subject must accept it use. Under the effect of hypnosis, the subject is more receptive to suggestions. In the hypnotic state, the subject has greater access to her/his subconscious mind, memories, and emotions.

In a nutshell, hypnosis is a state of deep relaxation of the whole nervous system. In the state of hypnosis, there is a change in body experience – namely, a decrease in the rate of respiration, a decrease in blood circulation and an altered brainwave state. When in a normal state of human consciousness, the subject's brain waves are at beta-wave level. However, under hypnosis, brain waves slow down to alpha-wave level and, then, to theta-wave state.

Use of hypnosis has been applied from the classroom to clinic, from public places to police station. The characteristics of hypnosis are great relaxation and deep concentration. Despite the fact that hypnosis is often misunderstood, it is highly intriguing. Hypnosis is not only popular, but it is also completely safe.

Hypnosis can be useful in treating a variety of human conditions – e.g., addictions, pain relief, weight control, fear reduction, and stopping smoking. The success of hypnosis depends greatly on the level of acceptance of the subject.

Under the effect of hypnosis, the subject gets accessibility to his subconscious mind – and its repressed memories. There are lots of misconceptions regarding hypnosis. Hypnosis is considered 'Black Magic' by some people. Hypnosis is regarded with the scientific certainty of brain-wave states by other people. Certainly, there are mixed reviews. But, for those who have experienced the powerful benefits of hypnosis, it is easy to affirm: Hypnosis exists.

What is hypnosis?

Hypnosis is a method that permits you to use both your own inner power and your own hidden capabilities (the capabilities that you may not even be aware that you possess). In addition,

• Hypnosis can help you reduce fears, phobias, and anxieties.

• Hypnosis can help you get rid of bad habits like unhealthy eating, smoking, biting nails, chewing snuff, drug addictions, etc.

What is hypnosis not?

• Hypnosis is **not** an experience of controlling another's mind: A hypnotist cannot use hypnosis to take control of your mind. Your permission is a must for hypnosis to occur.

• Hypnosis is **not** a tactic to make you reveal secrets.

• Hypnosis is **not** dangerous.

• Hypnosis is **not** weird of bizarre!

Some of the issues Hypnosis can be used for include:

1. Pain control
2. Weight management
3. Healthy eating
4. Habit cessation – e.g., stopping smoking, ceasing nail biting, exercising regularly, enjoying vegetables;
5. Overcoming phobias, fears & anxieties
6. A substitute for – or reduction of – anesthesia for medical procedures
7. And more, much more … (for more applications, cf. pg. 9)

Hypnosis can be beneficial if a viewpoint or some aspect of logical thinking becomes a barrier to solving a personal problem. Hypnosis can liberate you from problems, from which you have struggled on either a conscious or a subconscious level. Hypnosis can provide valuable assistance to improve the quality of one's life and the lives of others.

"Whatever the mind of man can conceive and believe,

it can achieve. Thoughts are things!

And powerful things at that ..."

-- Napoleon Hill

HYPNOSIS ESSENTIALS: THE POWER OF HYPNOSIS

Hundreds of studies have been conducted demonstrating that the power of hypnosis can be used to create amazing changes in your life – changes as diverse as eliminating pain to creating new behaviors. It has worked for millions of people in the past, continues to work for millions today, and has a high probability of working effectively for you, too!

Are you hypnotizable? Is there a possibility that YOU could enter into the deepest states of hypnotic trance? If you are an average-functioning human, it is highly likely that you can!

Many persons hold misperceptions about hypnosis. Some think that they cannot be hypnotized. Some people believe that to be hypnotized indicates a lack of real will-power or a below-level intelligence. These misconceptions are normal. They are also untrue.

Hypnosis is a natural state of mind. Humans go in and out of the hypnotic state many times each day.

The best hypnotic subjects are intelligent persons, who have a great deal of concentration, have a highly developed ability to focus and want to use hypnosis to accomplish an outcome in their lives. You should also be aware that the hypnotic state is different for each person who enters it. It is a state that can vary from individual to individual, and from session to session, with the same person.

Some people can enter extremely deep states of trance where their awareness completely changes and their memory of the event is hidden when they awaken. Others, when hypnotized, find themselves in a state that is equal to complete relaxation. Most of us fall somewhere in between these two extremes. Wherever you find yourself on the hypnotic trance-scale, one thing is for certain – since hypnosis is a natural state of mind, everyone who wants to do so is capable of being hypnotized to some degree.

As was mentioned above, you go into trance states repeatedly throughout the day. Have you ever been "going through the motions", just performing a task without any conscious effort. Have you noticed that you were thinking of something completely different while performing this task? This is an example of spontaneous hypnosis.

If you travel on the bus or train, have you found yourself day-dreaming or remembering past events and been so engrossed in your mental image that you lost track of time or your surroundings for awhile? This is another example of spontaneous hypnosis.

Have you watched a great movie and totally identified with the characters or got so lost in the plot that it was all you were focused on? Or, have you gotten to the end of a commercial and failed to be able to recall the product-focus for the advertisement?

If you can answer "yes" to any of these questions – and almost everyone can – then you have already experienced the state of trance.

Just entering a hypnotic trance can be very therapeutic in and of itself. As your body and mind relax, there is an easing of tension throughout your whole system. This is a beneficial, healing state for both the mind and the body.

However, the real power of the hypnosis comes from the suggestions and images that the hypnotist uses in this state. Such suggestions can easily, quickly, and permanently alter not only your behavior but also your dominant thinking about any subject you choose.

Through suggestion a hypnotist will often guide you into a mental rehearsal of the new behaviors. New feelings are often anchored to old memories. In addition, a visualized future event can be reinforced in order to retrain your mind and body to respond to past situations in an entirely different way.

So are YOU hypnotizable?

Research shows that the best hypnotic subjects are those people who can easily immerse themselves in any imagined event. This skill is one that many people in the self-improvement field strive hard to acquire.

Hypnotic subjects who can easily enter the deepest, conscious-altering states of trance are those than can easily become absorbed in a fantasy while blocking out their external surroundings. This basically means the better your imaginative abilities, the more profoundly you will experience the hypnotic state.

However, everyone can be hypnotized and you are no exception! Under the correct conditions, you most definitely can and will enter a state of trance. With the right stimuli, you can then use this state as catalyst for change in your life. It is possible to remove unwanted behaviors, instill new ones, and even program yourself with characteristics and personality traits that you desire.

You can use hypnosis to make changes in just about every area of your life. It can be used to heal you on all levels -- body, mind, emotions, and spirit.

Hypnotists have long found that its uses are almost endless! For example, UK hypnotist Paul McKenna hypnotized a man diagnosed with a form of hysterical blindness. The man's doctors believed a psychological trauma had caused the man's blindness and that his eyesight should be working perfectly.

After a few sessions with Hypnotist McKenna, the man's sight began to return and he was able to function more productively than before. This was remarkable!

Yet, even more fascinating still, before the program had finished shooting, the man was sent to an eyesight specialist who discovered that he had been wrongly diagnosed. In fact there had been substantial damage done to this man's visual equipment!

As far as medical science was concerned this man should not have been able to see anything! Yet, through hypnosis, his sight was dramatically improved. Why? Because both the hypnotist and the subject believed that it was possible. This is an example of how the subconscious mind creates what one believes to be real!

Here's a short list of areas where hypnosis can be used effectively. A comprehensive list would, literally, fill a book!:

a) Aid In relaxation
b) Weight Loss Hypnosis
c) Better Study Habits
d) Hypnosis for Insomnia
e) Pain Management
f) Eliminate Fears & Phobias
g) Alleviate Depression
h) Release Issues from the Past
i) Awaken Your Creativity
j) Create More Success
k) Improve Self Confidence Hypnosis
l) Past Life Regression
m) Improve Your Memory
n) Improve Your Sports Performance
o) Stop Smoking with Hypnosis
p) Elimination of Warts
q) Healing Of Skin Conditions
r) Reduce Anxiety & Stress
s) Change Habits
t) Remove Addictions
u) Self-help Hypnosis
v) Eliminate the Fear of Flying
w) Lucid Dreaming

Basically, the only limitations on hypnosis are those that the subject places on it! What do you think hypnosis might be able to do for YOU?

I invite you to use hypnosis for yourself! You have a whole new reality to gain!

"Your thoughts determine what you experience.

To change your life,

simply change your mind."

                    -- Dr. Lena Cather

HYPNOSIS ESSENTIALS: HYPNOSIS AND
THE AMAZING SUBCONSCIOUS MIND

The study of the human mind is a fascinating, extremely complex process of discovery. It is well-accepted-as-fact that the mind controls everything we say or do, think or feel.

It is also possible to feel a certain way, but not be able to explain why. When this occurs, it can seem as though one does not have the power to change the feelings, even though you might want to or know that you should.

Sadness or emotional pain of any kind is not typically a welcome feeling. But often one feels powerless to overcome it. Intense mental struggles can represent a battle between your conscious mind and your subconscious mind.

The conscious part of the mind is the part that you are aware of most of the time. The conscious mind processes thoughts and images that you acknowledge and affirm.

The conscious mind is the repository of your imagination and your creativity. However, the conscious mind is limited by what's around you. The conscious mind is restricted by what you are part of, and what you are exposed to.

Your subconscious mind is the part of your mind is the deep part of your mind. Your subconscious mind works silently on a deep level, behind the scenes. It processes and stores thoughts and images outside of your awareness; many times, it process and stores without your actual knowledge.

The subconscious mind is where the foundation – the fundamental core – of your beliefs, your views, your abilities, even your emotions and behaviors reside. Your subconscious mind is where you store your inner answers. It is the place you might refer to as "deep down". When you use that expression, you are basically stating it for what the subconscious mind truly is – a part of your mind that you know is there, yet, often, you are unaware of what it is doing or telling you.

You utilize your subconscious mind continually, often without ever realizing it. The subconscious mind is where your creative power really resides. It is the place where you can be influenced, affected, and moved emotionally.

However, if you are like many other persons, you may lack the ability to purposefully tap into your subconscious mind on your own.

Hypnosis can help you to do so!

Hypnosis takes you straight to the subconscious part of your mind. Once there, hypnosis allows you to tap into the subconscious mind.

Hypnosis allows you to add to the material that your subconscious mind brings into reality. Hypnosis allows you to remove counterproductive ideas from your subconscious mind. Hypnosis allows you to tap into the part of your mind

that holds your fundamental beliefs. It is at this level of
depth that hypnotic influence can be applied most effectively.

The hypnotic state helps you tap into the core of the matter.
Hypnosis then helps you identify what is in the subconscious
mind and bring it to a conscious level. At this level, you can
deal with the material more effectively.

Hypnosis, then, is directed at the subconscious mind, where
it can have the most benefit. Once you are back in your
waking state of mind, your subconscious mind carries out
the suggestions that you've been given while you were in the
hypnotic state.

"You – not outside events – have power

over your mind ..."

-- Marcus Aurelius

HYPNOSIS ESSENTIALS: 7 LAWS OF MIND

For effective hypnosis, it is important to be aware of certain Principles. If you are not aware of the following Seven Laws of Mind, you may end up creating the opposite of what you desire with your creative visualization and hypnosis/self-hypnosis practice.

Law #1: Law of Mind-Body Interaction

Every thought (mental) affects the body (physical). The mind and the body are usually seen as separate. However, this is far from the reality of the situation. In practice, the mind and body interact intimately.

For example, you can react to mental stress with knots in your back … or headaches … or ulcers. Because of this interaction, it is essential to be aware of your thoughts. If you are negative in your thoughts about yourself and your experiences, in essence, you subject yourself to negative self-hypnosis. Do not underestimate the severity of the effects of negative self-hypnosis! The effects will manifest as a physical reflection of whatever thoughts you had been thinking.

Law #2: Law of Desire

For successful change to occur in your life, you must TRULY want the outcome you claim to seek. It's not enough to just be passive and uninvolved in the outcome. It's not enough to want it just a little bit. For a positive outcome to occur, it is important to have invest it with emotion – to have a burning desire for that positive outcome!

Law #3: The Law of Expectation

What you expect tends to occur. When your mind TRULY believes and sincerely EXPECTS an outcome, the imagined result is very likely to happen. When you have faith and expectancy, beyond the shadow of a doubt, that you will get better, make more money, have a better relationship, etc. – stay vigilant! You will begin to witness yourself achieving that goal.

If you wake up telling yourself you will have a bad day, you probably will. In other words, your expectations drive your results. Negative expectations can provide the foundation for negative self-hypnosis … and negative results. Conversely, positive expectations provide the foundation for positive outcomes in your life.

Law #4: Law of Visualization

What is visualized – with energy and expectancy – powerfully manifests the envisioned result! When that visualization is positive, the respective end result will be positive. With guidance and skilled repetition, positive results can be consciously programmed.

Negatives can be released and new positive images can be imprinted. For the most effective results, it is important that you make the new positive image believable … as a part of reality of yourself and your life. Once you begin to easily see yourself becoming part of this believable new physical visual image, your subconscious mind steps in and begins to create that image as reality.

Law #5: The Law of Imagination

Imagination is stronger than knowledge. You 'know' that ghosts and monsters do not exist. Yet, hearing ghost stories at night still tends to create fear. This is especially true if the ghost stories are told while sitting around a campfire in a forest. There is no contest: Imagination will win out!

So, when you are thinking about the type of thoughts and visualizations to use in creative visualization and in hypnosis, remember the power and prevalence of imagination. This is a strong, compelling argument for the importance of positive thoughts and visualizations in your practice of self-hypnosis.

Law #6: Law of Repetition

For maximum positive outcome, repetition of the creative visualization, or of hypnosis, is vital. The importance of repetition cannot be understated. Humans are creatures of habit. To be successful in changing long-standing habits, it is important to get the message to your subconscious mind – the deep part of your mind – the very place where change occurs.

Repetition is the vehicle for getting images out of past memories, frameworks, and schemas. Repetition is the vehicle for getting new positive images into the programming dimensions of the subconscious. At this level, mind can be reprogrammed, or rewired. Repetition greatly increases the odds for the reprogramming to become permanent change.

Law #7: Law of Resistance

What you resist strongly, stays with you strongly. Have you ever had to stop doing something and found that its more difficult than you realized? Maybe you have had occasion to go on a diet and suddenly foods that you couldn't have cared less about prior to the diet start looking very appetizing?

Or, maybe there is someone who irritates you. Have you ever noticed that, even while you recognize that there is no reason for you to have this reaction, it seems that the more you try to keep the irritation away, it tends to get to you even more?

These examples could go on and on. Basically, when you resist something, it tends to stick even-more strongly. This happens because, when you resist, you end up thinking of the very thing you are trying to resist! As a result, it becomes continuously on your mind.

It's as if someone told you that, if you can go all day without thinking of a pink giraffe, they would give you $1000. I'm sure you don't usually spend your time thinking of something as random as a pink giraffe. However, trying to resist that image of a pink giraffe with the $1000 on the line would tend to be very difficult.

In other words, what you resist tends to stay with you. This being the case, when you are phrasing an affirmation – or a hypnotic suggestion – it is essential to phrase the affirmation in the positive. In other words, it is important to focus on what you want to create (not that which you desire to overcome). For example, you might use the affirmation, "I feel confident of success in accomplishing my goals!" You affirm what you want to achieve and NOT what you want to eliminate from your life!

By following these seven Laws of Mind, you soon discover that your day-to-day thoughts are guided in a positive direction. Now, since your thoughts create your internal emotional states, in essence, this is the same as self-hypnosis!

Truly, you hypnotize yourself frequently – and repeatedly – each and every day. Since you do, it is important to be consistently aware of your thoughts – and of keeping them positive! Since your subconscious mind creates that which you are thinking, by keeping your thoughts positive, you focus your mind to create what you most want to experience in your life.

"The only limitations on what you can do

are self-imposed. They are the

limitations of your own mind."

-- G. W. Mayfair

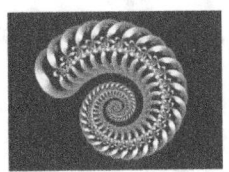

HYPNOSIS ESSENTIALS: MYTH vs. REALITY

Hollywood hype would have us believe that a hypnotist can control and direct our actions. The popular media suggests that we can be made to do all sorts of unimaginable things under hypnosis.

This chapter will look at some of the common myths about hypnosis – and the reality of the situation.

Myth #1: The hypnotist can make you do things against your will.

Reality #1: Absolutely False. The hypnotist has no powers over you at all. You – and you alone – are the person who accepts or rejects the suggestions that are given during your hypnosis session. The hypnotist cannot make you do things against your will.

All Hypnosis is really self-directed and self-controlled. There is a simple, true saying, "All hypnosis is self-hypnosis." The hypnotist merely guides you into a hypnotic state, and feeds your mind with carefully worded suggestions.

If you feel uncomfortable with any suggestions, you remain in charge of your own mind. This being the case, you may reject whatever suggestions you choose.

Hypnosis is essentially a matter of cooperation between the hypnotist and his subject. Hypnosis is not some form of power the hypnotist possesses; the hypnotist cannot compel the subject to submit to the hypnotist's will.

Myth #2: Once under Hypnosis, one can't come out of the state on his own.

Reality #2: If you are under hypnosis and the hypnotist suddenly left the room, two things may happen. You will either realize that the hypnotist is no longer talking to you, and will open your eyes, feeling fresh and alert.

Or, you might drift into natural sleep. In this case, you will awaken after a little while, as from normal sleep. So, you – the subject – comes out of the trance on your own.

Myth #3: Only weak-minded people can be hypnotized.

Reality #3: False. Hypnosis has nothing to do with will power. People often confuse hypnotizability with gullibility. There is no connection between the two.

On the contrary, in general, the more intelligent a person is, the easier it is for him to be hypnotized. To be hypnotized, one needs the abilities of concentration, imagination and vivid visualization.

Myth #4: Under hypnosis, the subject is totally unconscious.

Reality #4: At all times, during the course of a hypnotic session, you will be able to hear and to think. You are conscious. You are aware of what is going on around you. Although your body is very relaxed, your mind is actually more alert than usual.

Many people are worried by stage hypnosis. In stage hypnosis, the subjects – many of whom do ridiculous things during the session – seem to have no knowledge of anything around them. Such, however, can be easily demonstrated to not be the case. Unfortunately, though, stage hypnosis can convey an incorrect idea to observers, who might well be persons who could really benefit from hypnotherapy. These misperceptions may be so off-putting as to frightened and dissuade those who are afraid of losing control.

Myth #5: Under hypnosis, one can be made to reveal his secrets.

Reality #5: As mentioned above, under hypnosis, the subject is fully alert. In fact, under hypnosis, the subjects tend to be even-more alert than usual.

The hypnotist can be a guide for the subject – showing her/him the way to remember forgotten memories. Whether the subject reveals these to the hypnotist is entirely at his/her own discretion.

Myth #6: Hypnosis is dangerous.

Reality #6: Untrue. It is quite the opposite. Hypnosis is a safe and natural process.

We go in and out of hypnosis several times in our daily lives. For example, while driving along a highway, people have reported suddenly discovering that they have lost conscious awareness – that they were daydreaming – for several minutes at a time. This exemplifies spontaneous hypnotism.

Myth #7: One needs special powers to be hypnotized.

Reality #7: Any average person with the willingness and patience to learn can master the skills of hypnosis. Like other skills – such as playing the piano or learning a foreign language – some people are "naturals". They become accomplished with little training.

Through training and regular practice, others can increase their abilities with hypnosis. A good, confident voice can be a definite advantage; although, it is not a must.

While it is normal for adults to be hypnotized, children may lack an understanding and appreciation for the subject. Children below the age of 5 may not respond to hypnosis in the desired way. So, with young children, it might better to use other modalities for treatment.

Myth #8: The user might become dependent on hypnosis.

Reality #8: You cannot become dependent upon hypnosis because it has no negative, lasting physical effects on the body. While it is not a dependency, many people eagerly look forward to their daily hypnosis exercises.

They enjoy the time spent in deep relaxation. For these persons, hypnosis has stressing-reducing benefits. Frequent hypnosis induction provides an experience of peace and well-being, from which the hypnotic subjects awaken refreshed.

"Once you become aware of your feelings
as they really are
and not as you imagine them to be,
you step into true control.

For you have broken their **hypnotic** *lock on your life."*

-- G. W. Mayfair

HYPNOSIS ESSENTIALS: SUSCEPTIBILITY TO HYPNOSIS

A person's susceptibility to hypnosis depends on several variables. Whether these variables work together or are at cross-purposes to each other is entirely in the hands of the individual.

Some of these factors are outside of anyone's control. These factors rely on the individual makeup of each person.

For instance, if someone is naturally susceptible to suggestion in their everyday life, they likely will also carry that susceptibility through in hypnosis. Everyone is susceptible to some degree, but the greater the susceptibility of the hypnotic subject, the greater the likelihood of the subject's easily achieving hypnosis.

There are varying degrees of depth of hypnosis. In fact, effective hypnotherapy does not require a deep state of hypnosis. Hypnotherapy can be totally beneficial even at very-light levels.

Susceptibility to suggestion is also impacted by increased repetition. The more you hear a message, the more likely you will be to able accept it as fact. The more often you listen to suggestion, the more probable it is that you will accept it, whether consciously or not.

This is also true in everyday life.

Some people take to hypnosis quite effortlessly, while others need a bit more practice. The degree of susceptibility of the latter might be influenced by other conditions around them. In addition, they may find they need conducive circumstances – low distraction level, soft lighting, etc. – to achieve hypnosis.

But the most important contributor to someone's susceptibility to hypnosis is his/her attitude. If a person tries hypnosis and has immediate success, that's terrific. This can reinforce their continued ease in experiencing the hypnotic state. But, if someone tries hypnosis and struggles with it, some people will stop and conclude that hypnosis doesn't work. This is an unfortunate conclusion.

Hypnosis is a conditioning exercise. This means that it is easier to go into hypnosis and to go deeper on second and subsequent sessions.

If someone stops too soon, they run the risk of preventing themselves from getting the benefits. They short-stop themselves – they keep themselves from learning how easily, and how effectively, hypnosis could work for them.

The effectiveness of hypnosis relies on suggestion. Certainly, there is a degree of suggestion to all forms of therapy. For hypnosis, though, the major prerequisite for hypnosis candidacy is, first and foremost, attitude.

Certainly, other intellectual variances may factor in – variables such as concentration and imagination. However, these would be more likely to affect the depth of hypnosis, rather than the ability to achieve hypnosis.

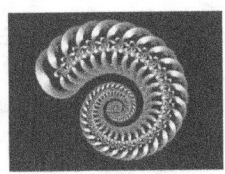

HYPNOSIS ESSENTIALS: 9 SURPRISING USES FOR HYPNOSIS

You're probably aware of people who stop smoking with hypnosis or who lose weight with hypnosis. Possibly, you have even heard how hypnosis can help explore past memories.

That's not all where hypnosis is concerned!

Here are some things hypnosis can help you do that might surprise or amaze you:

Secret #1: Get More Done in Less Time

Time management is definitely not all about organizing your files or upgrading your technology. Productivity, effectiveness, and enjoying what you do all start in your mind – specifically, in your subconscious mind.

How best to access your subconscious mind? Yes, hypnosis IS the answer here!

Surprise #2: Locate Lost Objects

If you have some knowledge of the object's whereabouts – even if you cannot consciously remember – that knowledge, hypnosis can help! Perhaps, you were the one who put the misplaced object away. Or, perhaps you witnessed the object being put away. In either case – even if the incident occurred years ago – hypnosis may help. Give it a try and see what happens.

Surprise #3: Exercise Longer, Stronger and More Enjoyably

Hypnosis can help you turn distaste for working out into a craving. Ask yourself: "What would exercising give me? What would it make possible in my life?"

A talented hypnotherapist spins a powerful motivational story for your subconscious mind. S/he makes it all so desirable that you can't wait to shop for – and break in – new running shoes.

Surprise #4: Enjoy Foods You've Previously Avoided

Nutritionists tell you that brussel sprouts are healthy, and whole-grain bread is better for you than white. But what if you just don't like the taste of brussel sprouts and whole-grain bread? Or, what if you detest the taste of all vegetables?

A little hypnosis might help you change all that. 'Give it a try! Note: If your resistance persists, have your hypnotist check for an allergy. Sometimes, your body just "knows."

Surprise #5: End Cravings

This is the reverse of #4. Using hypnosis can help helps you turn down brownies, stop uncontrolled shopping, or, even, let go of a lingering relationship to which you have been hanging on and hanging on.

Secret #6: Transform Your Dental Experience

For many persons, visiting the dentist is a source of worry, stress, and anxiety. Apprehensive patients quickly learn to associate feelings of fear and discomfort with dentistry. Future dental treatments then act as a trigger for these feelings whether they are appropriate or not. Using hypnosis, negative emotional associations – those that had been associated with dentistry – can be eliminated. Using hypnosis, negative emotional cues can be changed to positive feelings and behaviors.

In addition to this, hypnosis has also been demonstrated to
(a) reduce the experience of dental pain;
(b) increase the level of relaxation in the dental chair;
(c) reduce both bleeding and the amount of required
      anesthetic; and
(d) accelerate healing

This improved dental experience can also stimulate the patient to strive for better oral hygiene and a more-regular treatment schedule.

Surprise #7: Enjoy Public Speaking

The fear of public speaking is sometimes referred to as a greater fear than death. This is really too bad. Being an effective speaker can boost your career in your company, your industry, and beyond.

Enter hypnosis … Once-reticent clients are astounded at the changes in themselves – and the benefits they reap – from using hypnosis to conquer this fear. Where using hypnosis to stop smoking stops draining money, using hypnosis to become a good speaker puts money in the bank. Hypnosis can help you accomplish both!

Secret #8: Attract Your Life Partner

Do you believe that finding the person of your dreams is about mesmerizing that other – most desirable – person? No, not so. Finding the person of your dreams starts with yourself!

Hypnosis for confidence, sex appeal, and/or warm, intimate rapport can give you a feeling you've never had before. This sense of self proves to be very appealing to others, especially that special person of your dreams.

Why not try it out for yourself?

Secret #9: Relieve an itch

Really. When is an itch not an itch? An itch is not an itch when it's a habit. Keep scratching some itches and they feel itchier.

And irritated.

Irritated skin often itches (not to mention bleeds), so you've created a cycle. Via hypnosis, you can tell your subconscious
 (1) to disengage from the phantom itching;
 (2) to allow your total healing; and
 (3) to return your skin to healthy, comfortable smoothness.

"Home is where the heart is ...

Love provides the backdrop of confidence

and self-esteem to guide you home.

-- Dr. Anna Wayne

HYPNOSIS ESSENTIALS: CREATIVE VISUALIZATION
12 STEPS TO MIND POWER

These 12 steps to Creative Visualization are intended to
(a) focus and generate Mind Power;
(b) build positive visuals;
(c) serve as an powerful preliminary exercise to hypnosis
Your wants, desires, wishes, and dreams may be as varied
as improving your personality, increasing your wealth,
attracting love, or making yourself more attractive. Whatever
your dreams and desires may be, Creative Visualization is
an intensely powerful technique to bring them into reality!

I invite you to follow these steps in the Power of Creative
Visualization:

Step #1: Choose a Quiet Place

This Quiet Place is one that is, preferably, free from all
distraction, interruption or disturbance. This Place may be
inside a bus or in your own room. The ideal is that you find a
suitable Place of your choosing, that enables you to
concentrate easily and fully. The ideal place may be
anywhere as long as you can focus and concentrate there.

Step #2: Be Comfortable

Wear loose clothing, or loosen your belt and tie; remove tight jewelry, etc.

Step #3: Let Yourself Relax

Keep your spine straight. Loosen your hands – this eases your body tension and helps your blood circulate efficiently. Relax!

Step #4: Close Your Eyes

By closing your eyes, you prevent the external, physical world from interrupting you. As a result, you can concentrate on your inner, mental-emotional-spiritual world. Avoid squinting or tightening your eyes. Close them gently. In fact, once you focus on your images, you may find your eyes closing naturally.

Step #5: Breathe Deeply & Slowly

Let your body roll with the rhythm of your breathing. Listen to that rhythm. Allow it to become gradually slower and deeper. Allow yourself to move with your breathing into deeper levels of relaxation and restfulness.

Step #6: Begin the Process of Visualization

Create the key images of the subject you have chosen. Form the shape. Add color. Build the sound. Sense them! Focus on them. See them as sharply and clearly as you can with your mind's eye.

Step #7: Insert Yourself

Put yourself in the images you have created. Put yourself inside the picture. By doing so, you let your subconscious mind know that the image you see that leads to your goal is meant specifically for you. You clearly convey to your subconscious mind that these images are not for anyone else.

Step #8: Feel the Image

Now that you are inside the picture, imagine yourself taking the lead. Feel the environment. Use all of your senses -- allow your images to come alive! Watch how differently it looks to lead a life that you desire! Notice how it feels to lead the life that you desire. Feel it as REAL in your life ... right here, right now!

Step #9: Let Your Emotions Go

See! Hear! Smell! Feel! Sense how it is to achieve your goals. Let the excitement and happiness of success flow through you. Let the thrill of success build in you. Feel your own success!

Step #10: Let Your Mind Become Blank

As you let your mind go blank, imagine that you are releasing this newly envisioned – emotionally-charged – reality into the Universe. Imagine that you are letting it go into that space of Creativity where it becomes manifest. So, let go of the images and experience of your new reality.

Step #11: Create the Mental Space to Receive

Tell yourself specifically what you desire – for example, "I desire to be healthy", "I deserve to be rich and famous." By doing this, you not only let your subconscious mind support the picture, you literally pave the way through your words – those totally-creative words – to achieve your success.

Step #12: Feel the Creativity

While you create these images, feel your own creativity flooding throughout your being. Pay attention as you begin to resonate with the images and sensations that you created. Feel them becoming more and more real – more and more a part of YOUR reality!

These 12 Steps provide the foundational guidelines to create the visuals that will help you achieve your goals. You may change them to more-effectively suit your needs. The more precisely the images meet your specific needs, the more effective they will be.

These (preceding) are the Twelve important Steps to Mind Power. It is better to visualize 2-3 times a day for 10 minutes, than it is to visualize for a long stretch during the day. Doing this helps the quality of the visuals remain fresh. They neither become stale nor drain energy from you.

Steps #1 to #12 might take you between 5-10 minutes. It is better to not prolong it. Instead, repeat it at two other times per day.

When you release the image after this brief exercise, your conscious mind becomes free of the Mind Power you have activated. Your subconscious mind, however, keeps on supporting the image(s) that you envisioned through visualization. These help your goal and your dreams to more quickly become a reality.

These Twelve Steps to Mind Power are the most powerful tool in the world! When you switch on your Mind Power and extend it to Creative Visualization, YOU TURN YOUR DREAMS INTO REALITY!

Remember: It is YOUR mind – by using it effectively, you can rule the world. Creative Visualization is an exceptional place to start!

When you are ready to do so, you can add the intensity of the hypnotic state to the preliminary practice that these Creative Visualization exercises have accomplished for you. To do so, engage the services of a professional hypnotist to achieve expert results in your life!

"The greatest discovery of my generation is that a human being can alter his life by altering his attitudes of mind."

-- William James

SUMMARY & BEYOND

If you have been unhappy with your life, now is a **great time** to begin to use hypnosis to assist you to change. Steps to facilitate this change include:

1. Create a positive scenario about your life. Include visualization of the desired change already having been made. Since your subconscious mind creates that which you are thinking, actively enlist your subconscious – by using the following Laws of Mind – to activate results quickly & effectively:

2. **Law of Desire** – Intensify your desire for your desired change; allow yourself to actually feel how much you want your life to be happier, to be better

3. **Law of Expectation** – Energize your expectations of bringing that change quickly and effectively into your life

4. **Law of Visualization** – Use the Creative Visualization exercise on the results indicated in your positive scenario

5. **Law of Imagination** – Use your imagination creatively and actively to energize your desired results; imagine your scenario as a part of your life … right now!

6. **Law of Repetition** – Repeat your Creative Visualization of your positive scenario ... See, hear, taste, smell, touch the results as a part of your life

7. **Law of Mind-Body Interaction** – Imagine that your positive visualization, which begins with your mind, now expands to include successful changes in your body. Imagine yourself enjoying these changes – physically – on an everyday basis.

8. Now release these results to the creative forces of the Universe and allow them to enter your life ... starting this very moment!

To help you on your way even more effectively, I've included a series of Worksheets to guide you in taking these steps toward living your dreams. I encourage you to get started on using – and benefiting from – them. I invite you to get started Right Now. Your dreams are just waiting for you to enjoy!

You *can* do it!!

You *can* do it!!

I *can* do it!!!

HYPNOSIS ESSENTIALS

WORKSHEETS

HYPNOSIS ESSENTIALS WORKSHEETS

Affirmative Statements

Write affirmative statements for yourself – statements about the new reality of your dreams. State these affirmative statements in the present tense, as though they were already occurring in your life:

_____ 1.

_____ 2.

_____ 3.

_____ 4.

_____ 5.

_____ 6.

_____ 7.

_____ 8.

_____ 9.

_____10.

HYPNOSIS ESSENTIALS WORKSHEETS

Priority List

Go back to your list on the previous page and prioritize the affirmations in the order in which you would most like to see these ideas manifested in your life.

Use the blank at the beginning of the line for listing your priority-list ranking numbers.

HYPNOSIS ESSENTIALS WORKSHEETS

Re-examination

Re-examine your list on page 29. With the priority listing that you have now established, are your affirmative statements listed in the order in which you would most like to see the affirmative ideas manifested in your life?

If so, re-write your list below according to its current priority listings:

1.

2.

3.

4.

5.

6.

7.

8.

9.

10.

HYPNOSIS ESSENTIALS WORKSHEETS

Creative Visualization Exercise #1

Use the Affirmative Statement that you listed on your Priority List as #1.

Initiate a Creative Visualization Session and focus on this affirmation as the theme for your Visualization Creativity. Review pages 41 to 48 to refresh your memory about how to engage in Creative Visualization. Remember it only takes 5' to 10' each time; we'll just focus on 1 session per day.

Remember: See it! Hear it! Taste it! Touch it! Feel it! Be it!

After you have completed your Creative Visualization Exercise #1, note any impressions and awareness that you came to you during the exercise. Also note any thoughts or ideas that came to mind – these can give you insight into ways to be more successful in bringing your affirmative statement to life – an enjoyable part of your Reality:

Creative Visualization – as does Hypnosis – works best with repetition. Repeat your Creative Visualization Exercise for Affirmation #1 for 5 days. Doing so will "seal in" successful manifestation of Affirmation #1.

Use the Affirmative Statement that you listed on your Priority List as #1.

Initiate a Creative Visualization Session and focus on this affirmation as the theme for your Visualization Creativity. If you need to do so, review pages 41 to 48 to refresh your memory about how to engage in Creative Visualization.

Remember: See it! Hear it! Taste it! Touch it! Feel it! Be it!

After you have completed this repeat of Creative Visualization Exercise #2, note any additional impressions and awareness, thought or ideas that came to mind – these can give you insight into ways to be more successful in bringing your affirmative statement to life – an enjoyable part of your Reality. If you need more space, please use additional sheets?:

Notes for Creative Visualization #2 for Affirmation #1:

Notes for Creative Visualization #3 for Affirmation #1:

Notes for Creative Visualization #4 for Affirmation #1:

Notes for Creative Visualization #5 for Affirmation #1:

HYPNOSIS ESSENTIALS WORKSHEETS

Creative Visualization Exercise #2

Use the Affirmative Statement that you listed on your Priority List as #2.

Initiate a Creative Visualization Session and focus on this affirmation as the theme for your Visualization Creativity. If you wish to do so, review pages 41 to 48 to refresh your memory about how to engage in Creative Visualization.

Remember: See it! Hear it! Taste it! Touch it! Feel it! Be it!

After you have completed your Creative Visualization Exercise #2, note any impressions and awareness that you came to you during the exercise. Also note any thoughts or ideas that came to mind – these can give you insight into ways to be more successful in bringing your affirmative statement to life – an enjoyable part of your Reality:

Creative Visualization – as does Hypnosis – works best with repetition. Repeat your Creative Visualization Exercise for Affirmation #2 for 5 days. Doing so will "seal in" successful manifestation of Affirmation #2

HYPNOSIS ESSENTIALS WORKSHEETS
Creative Visualization Exercise #2 (Cont'd)

Use the Affirmative Statement that you listed on your Priority List as #2.

Initiate a Creative Visualization Session and focus on this affirmation as the theme for your Visualization Creativity. If you wish, review pages 41 to 48 to refresh your memory about how to engage in Creative Visualization.

Remember: See it! Hear it! Taste it! Touch it! Feel it! Be it!

After you have completed this repeat of Creative Visualization Exercise #2, note any additional impressions and awareness, thought or ideas that came to mind – these can give you insight into ways to be more successful in bringing your affirmative statement to life – an enjoyable part of your Reality. If you need more space, please use additional sheets?:

Notes for Creative Visualization #2 for Affirmation #2:

Notes for Creative Visualization #3 for Affirmation #2:

Notes for Creative Visualization #4 for Affirmation #2:

Notes for Creative Visualization #5 for Affirmation #2:

HYPNOSIS ESSENTIALS WORKSHEETS

Creative Visualization Exercise #3

Use the Affirmative Statement that you listed on your Priority List as #3.

Initiate a Creative Visualization Session and focus on this affirmation as the theme for your Visualization Creativity. If you wish to do so, review pages 41 to 48 to refresh your memory about how to engage in Creative Visualization.

Remember: See it! Hear it! Taste it! Touch it! Feel it! Be it!

After you have completed your Creative Visualization Exercise #3, note any impressions and awareness that you came to you during the exercise. Also note any thoughts or ideas that came to mind – these can give you insight into ways to be more successful in bringing your affirmative statement to life – an enjoyable part of your Reality:

Creative Visualization – as does Hypnosis – works best with repetition. Repeat your Creative Visualization Exercise for Affirmation #3 for 5 days. Doing so will "seal in" successful manifestation of Affirmation #3.

Use the Affirmative Statement that you listed on your Priority List as #3.

Initiate a Creative Visualization Session and focus on this affirmation as the theme for your Visualization Creativity. If you wish, review pages 41 to 48 to refresh your memory about how to engage in Creative Visualization.

Remember: See it! Hear it! Taste it! Touch it! Feel it! Be it!

After you have completed this repeat of Creative Visualization Exercise #3, note any additional impressions and awareness, thought or ideas that came to mind – these can give you insight into ways to be more successful in bringing your affirmative statement to life – an enjoyable part of your Reality. If you need more space, please use additional sheets?:

Notes for Creative Visualization #2 for Affirmation #3:

Notes for Creative Visualization #3 for Affirmation #3:

Notes for Creative Visualization #4 for Affirmation #3:

Notes for Creative Visualization #5 for Affirmation #3:

HYPNOSIS ESSENTIALS WORKSHEETS

Creative Visualization Exercise #4

Use the Affirmative Statement that you listed on your Priority List as #4.

Initiate a Creative Visualization Session and focus on this affirmation as the theme for your Visualization Creativity. If you wish to do so, review pages 41 to 48 to refresh your memory about how to engage in Creative Visualization.

Remember: See it! Hear it! Taste it! Touch it! Feel it! Be it!

After you have completed your Creative Visualization Exercise #4, note any impressions and awareness that you came to you during the exercise. Also note any thoughts or ideas that came to mind – these can give you insight into ways to be more successful in bringing your affirmative statement to life – an enjoyable part of your Reality:

Creative Visualization – as does Hypnosis – works best with repetition. Repeat your Creative Visualization Exercise for Affirmation #4 for 5 days. Doing so will "seal in" successful manifestation of Affirmation #4.

Use the Affirmative Statement that you listed on your Priority List as #4.

Initiate a Creative Visualization Session and focus on this affirmation as the theme for your Visualization Creativity. If you wish, review pages 41 to 48 to refresh your memory about how to engage in Creative Visualization.

Remember: See it! Hear it! Taste it! Touch it! Feel it! Be it!

After you have completed this repeat of Creative Visualization Exercise #4, note any additional impressions and awareness, thought or ideas that came to mind – these can give you insight into ways to be more successful in bringing your affirmative statement to life – an enjoyable part of your Reality. If you need more space, please use additional sheets?:

Notes for Creative Visualization #2 for Affirmation #4:

Notes for Creative Visualization #3 for Affirmation #4:

Notes for Creative Visualization #4 for Affirmation #4:

Notes for Creative Visualization #5 for Affirmation #4:

HYPNOSIS ESSENTIALS WORKSHEETS

Creative Visualization Exercise #5

Use the Affirmative Statement that you listed on your Priority List as #5.

Initiate a Creative Visualization Session and focus on this affirmation as the theme for your Visualization Creativity. If you wish to do so, review pages 41 to 48 to refresh your memory about how to engage in Creative Visualization.

Remember: See it! Hear it! Taste it! Touch it! Feel it! Be it!

After you have completed your Creative Visualization Exercise #5, note any impressions and awareness that you came to you during the exercise. Also note any thoughts or ideas that came to mind – these can give you insight into ways to be more successful in bringing your affirmative statement to life – an enjoyable part of your Reality:

Creative Visualization – as does Hypnosis – works best with repetition. Repeat your Creative Visualization Exercise for Affirmation #5 for 5 days. Doing so will "seal in" successful manifestation of Affirmation #5.

HYPNOSIS ESSENTIALS WORKSHEETS
Creative Visualization Exercise #5 (Cont'd)

Use the Affirmative Statement that you listed on your Priority List as #5.

Initiate a Creative Visualization Session and focus on this affirmation as the theme for your Visualization Creativity. If you wish, review pages 41 to 48 to refresh your memory about how to engage in Creative Visualization.

Remember: See it! Hear it! Taste it! Touch it! Feel it! Be it!

After you have completed this repeat of Creative Visualization Exercise #5, note any additional impressions and awareness, thought or ideas that came to mind – these can give you insight into ways to be more successful in bringing your affirmative statement to life – an enjoyable part of your Reality. If you need more space, please use additional sheets?:

Notes for Creative Visualization #2 for Affirmation #5:

Notes for Creative Visualization #3 for Affirmation #5:

Notes for Creative Visualization #4 for Affirmation #5:

Notes for Creative Visualization #5 for Affirmation #5:

HYPNOSIS ESSENTIALS WORKSHEETS

Creative Visualization Exercise #6

Use the Affirmative Statement that you listed on your Priority List as #6.

Initiate a Creative Visualization Session and focus on this affirmation as the theme for your Visualization Creativity. If you wish to do so, review pages 41 to 48 to refresh your memory about how to engage in Creative Visualization.

Remember: See it! Hear it! Taste it! Touch it! Feel it! Be it!

After you have completed your Creative Visualization Exercise #6, note any impressions and awareness that you came to you during the exercise. Also note any thoughts or ideas that came to mind – these can give you insight into ways to be more successful in bringing your affirmative statement to life – an enjoyable part of your Reality:

Creative Visualization – as does Hypnosis – works best with repetition. Repeat your Creative Visualization Exercise for Affirmation #6 for 5 days. Doing so will "seal in" successful manifestation of Affirmation #6.

HYPNOSIS ESSENTIALS WORKSHEETS
Creative Visualization Exercise #6 (Cont'd)

Use the Affirmative Statement that you listed on your Priority List as #6.

Initiate a Creative Visualization Session and focus on this affirmation as the theme for your Visualization Creativity. If you wish, review pages 41 to 48 to refresh your memory about how to engage in Creative Visualization.

Remember: See it! Hear it! Taste it! Touch it! Feel it! Be it!

After you have completed this repeat of Creative Visualization Exercise #6, note any additional impressions and awareness, thought or ideas that came to mind – these can give you insight into ways to be more successful in bringing your affirmative statement to life – an enjoyable part of your Reality. If you need more space, please use additional sheets?:

Notes for Creative Visualization #2 for Affirmation #6:

Notes for Creative Visualization #3 for Affirmation #6:

Notes for Creative Visualization #4 for Affirmation #6:

Notes for Creative Visualization #5 for Affirmation #6:

HYPNOSIS ESSENTIALS WORKSHEETS

Creative Visualization Exercise #7

Use the Affirmative Statement that you listed on your Priority List as #7.

Initiate a Creative Visualization Session and focus on this affirmation as the theme for your Visualization Creativity. If you wish to do so, review pages 41 to 48 to refresh your memory about how to engage in Creative Visualization.

Remember: See it! Hear it! Taste it! Touch it! Feel it! Be it!

After you have completed your Creative Visualization Exercise #7, note any impressions and awareness that you came to you during the exercise. Also note any thoughts or ideas that came to mind – these can give you insight into ways to be more successful in bringing your affirmative statement to life – an enjoyable part of your Reality:

Creative Visualization – as does Hypnosis – works best with repetition. Repeat your Creative Visualization Exercise for Affirmation #7 for 5 days. Doing so will "seal in" successful manifestation of Affirmation #7.

Use the Affirmative Statement that you listed on your Priority List as #7.

Initiate a Creative Visualization Session and focus on this affirmation as the theme for your Visualization Creativity. If you wish, review pages 41 to 48 to refresh your memory about how to engage in Creative Visualization.

Remember: See it! Hear it! Taste it! Touch it! Feel it! Be it!

After you have completed this repeat of Creative Visualization Exercise #7, note any additional impressions and awareness, thought or ideas that came to mind – these can give you insight into ways to be more successful in bringing your affirmative statement to life – an enjoyable part of your Reality. If you need more space, please use additional sheets?:

Notes for Creative Visualization #2 for Affirmation #7:

Notes for Creative Visualization #3 for Affirmation #7:

Notes for Creative Visualization #4 for Affirmation #7:

Notes for Creative Visualization #5 for Affirmation #7:

HYPNOSIS ESSENTIALS WORKSHEETS

Creative Visualization Exercise #8

Use the Affirmative Statement that you listed on your Priority List as #8.

Initiate a Creative Visualization Session and focus on this affirmation as the theme for your Visualization Creativity. If you wish to do so, review pages 41 to 48 to refresh your memory about how to engage in Creative Visualization.

Remember: See it! Hear it! Taste it! Touch it! Feel it! Be it!

After you have completed your Creative Visualization Exercise #8, note any impressions and awareness that you came to you during the exercise. Also note any thoughts or ideas that came to mind – these can give you insight into ways to be more successful in bringing your affirmative statement to life – an enjoyable part of your Reality:

Creative Visualization – as does Hypnosis – works best with repetition. Repeat your Creative Visualization Exercise for Affirmation #8 for 5 days. Doing so will "seal in" successful manifestation of Affirmation #8.

Use the Affirmative Statement that you listed on your Priority List as #8.

Initiate a Creative Visualization Session and focus on this affirmation as the theme for your Visualization Creativity. If you wish, review pages 41 to 48 to refresh your memory about how to engage in Creative Visualization.

Remember: See it! Hear it! Taste it! Touch it! Feel it! Be it!

After you have completed this repeat of Creative Visualization Exercise #8, note any additional impressions and awareness, thought or ideas that came to mind – these can give you insight into ways to be more successful in bringing your affirmative statement to life – an enjoyable part of your Reality. If you need more space, please use additional sheets?:

Notes for Creative Visualization #2 for Affirmation #8:

Notes for Creative Visualization #3 for Affirmation #8:

Notes for Creative Visualization #4 for Affirmation #8:

Notes for Creative Visualization #5 for Affirmation #8:

HYPNOSIS ESSENTIALS WORKSHEETS

Creative Visualization Exercise #9

Use the Affirmative Statement that you listed on your Priority List as #9.

Initiate a Creative Visualization Session and focus on this affirmation as the theme for your Visualization Creativity. If you wish to do so, review pages 41 to 48 to refresh your memory about how to engage in Creative Visualization.

Remember: See it! Hear it! Taste it! Touch it! Feel it! Be it!

After you have completed your Creative Visualization Exercise #9, note any impressions and awareness that you came to you during the exercise. Also note any thoughts or ideas that came to mind – these can give you insight into ways to be more successful in bringing your affirmative statement to life – an enjoyable part of your Reality:

Creative Visualization – as does Hypnosis – works best with repetition. Repeat your Creative Visualization Exercise for Affirmation #9 for 5 days. Doing so will "seal in" successful manifestation of Affirmation #9.

Use the Affirmative Statement that you listed on your Priority List as #9.

Initiate a Creative Visualization Session and focus on this affirmation as the theme for your Visualization Creativity. If you wish, review pages 41 to 48 to refresh your memory about how to engage in Creative Visualization.

Remember: See it! Hear it! Taste it! Touch it! Feel it! Be it!

After you have completed this repeat of Creative Visualization Exercise #9, note any additional impressions and awareness, thought or ideas that came to mind – these can give you insight into ways to be more successful in bringing your affirmative statement to life – an enjoyable part of your Reality. If you need more space, please use additional sheets?:

Notes for Creative Visualization #2 for Affirmation #9:

Notes for Creative Visualization #3 for Affirmation #9:

Notes for Creative Visualization #4 for Affirmation #9:

Notes for Creative Visualization #5 for Affirmation #9:

HYPNOSIS ESSENTIALS WORKSHEETS

Creative Visualization Exercise #10

Use the Affirmative Statement that you listed on your Priority List as #10.

Initiate a Creative Visualization Session and focus on this affirmation as the theme for your Visualization Creativity. If you wish to do so, review pages 41 to 48 to refresh your memory about how to engage in Creative Visualization.

Remember: See it! Hear it! Taste it! Touch it! Feel it! Be it!

After you have completed your Creative Visualization Exercise #10, note any impressions and awareness that you came to you during the exercise. Also note any thoughts or ideas that came to mind – these can give you insight into ways to be more successful in bringing your affirmative statement to life – an enjoyable part of your Reality:

Creative Visualization – as does Hypnosis – works best with repetition. Repeat your Creative Visualization Exercise for Affirmation #10 for 5 days. Doing so will "seal in" successful manifestation of Affirmation #10.

Use the Affirmative Statement that you listed on your Priority List as #10.

Initiate a Creative Visualization Session and focus on this affirmation as the theme for your Visualization Creativity. If you wish, review pages 41 to 48 to refresh your memory about how to engage in Creative Visualization.

Remember: See it! Hear it! Taste it! Touch it! Feel it! Be it!

After you have completed this repeat of Creative Visualization Exercise #10 note any additional impressions and awareness, thought or ideas that came to mind – these can give you insight into ways to be more successful in bringing your affirmative statement to life – an enjoyable part of your Reality. If you need more space, please use additional sheets?:

Notes for Creative Visualization #2 for Affirmation #10:

Notes for Creative Visualization #3 for Affirmation #10:

Notes for Creative Visualization #4 for Affirmation #10:

Notes for Creative Visualization #5 for Affirmation #10:

"He who looks outside, dreams;

he who looks within, awakens."

-- Carl Jung

Greetings,

This is Dr. Marlene Shiple, the Life Coach Dr. I want to thank you sincerely for your interest in <u>Hypnosis</u> <u>Essentials</u>. I hope you found it intriguing, usable, *and* informative!

In addition, it is my fond hope that you treated yourself to completing the Creative Visualization Exercises and Worksheets on the previous pages. Investing your energy in this undertaking – and doing so FOR YOU – can speed up your progress toward creating the Life – the Reality – of your Dreams!

If you are reading this and have not yet completed the "worksheet" sections, I invite you to go back and do so now! I assure that it takes only a brief amount of time each day! For investing your time and energy in this way, I give you the following certainty: What you invest to create changes in Your Life, earns you massive benefits, benefits in proportion to your investment. YOU – and **you** alone – are the A-#1, All-time WINNER!

I encourage you to invest for the WIN. YOU are worth it!!

Warm regards,

Marlene Shiple, Ph.D.

The Life Coach Dr.

"By accepting yourself fully, exactly the way you are right now, you become free to change."

-- Dr. Anna Wayne

To learn more about Hypnosis and to view
our Extensive selection of Hypnosis-CD-
Workbook Programs, kindly visit us at
http://thelifecoachdr.com/coach
and click on Coaching Products (All)

Marlene Shiple, Ph.D.
The Life Coach Dr.
http://thelifecoachdr.com/coach
(602) 266 – 6662

To select from our Extensive selection
Hypnosis-CD-plus-Workbook Programs,
come and visit at http://thelifecoachdr.com/coach
then click on Coaching Products (All)

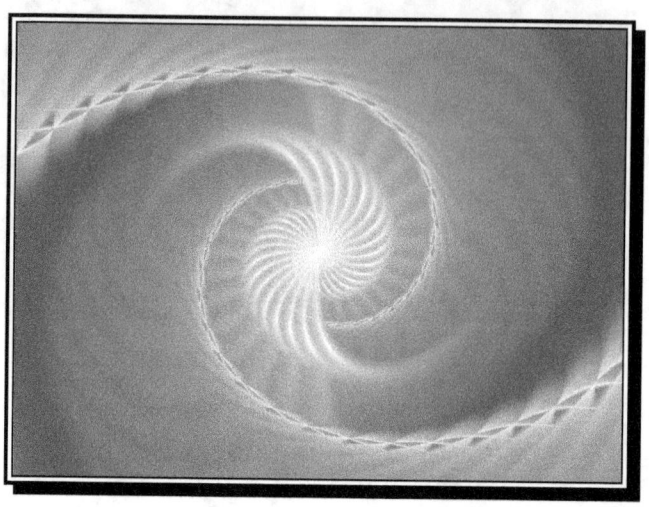

Marlene Shiple, Ph.D.
The Life Coach Dr.
http://thelifecoachdr.com/coach
(602) 266 – 6662

www.ingramcontent.com/pod-product-compliance
Lightning Source LLC
Chambersburg PA
CBHW062103280526
45788CB00003B/1334